Afraid of the Water
PORTUGUESE MAN-of-WAR
Floating Misery

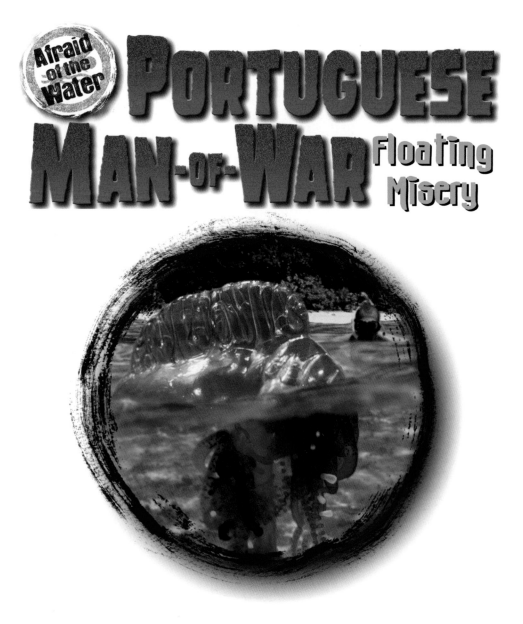

by Natalie Lunis

Consultant: James B. Wood, Ph.D.
Director of Education at the Aquarium of the Pacific
Long Beach, California

BEARPORT
PUBLISHING

New York, New York

Credits

Cover and Title Page, © Ralf Kiefner/SeaPics and rest/iStockphoto; 5, © Oxford Scientific/Photolibrary; 6, © Norbert Rehm/Shutterstock; 7, © Douglas R. Clifford/St. Petersburg Times; 8, © Ralf Kiefner/SeaPics; 9, © Chris Howey/Shutterstock; 10, © Peter Parks/Image Quest Marine; 11, © Peter Parks/IQ3-D/SeaPics; 13T, © Kelvin Aitken/Peter Arnold Inc.; 13B, © João Ricardo; 14, © bitis73/ImageVortex; 15, © Kathie Atkinson/Auscape International; 16L, © Kim Bunker/iStockphoto; 16R, © Phillip Colla/SeaPics; 17T, © Georgette Douwma/PhotoResearchers, Inc.; 17B, © Peter Parks/Image Quest Marine; 18, © Henrique Daniel Araujo/Shutterstock; 19, © Norbert Wu/Minden Pictures; 20, © AP Images/The Standard-Times/Peter Pereira; 21T, © Roy Morsch/age fotostock/Photolibrary; 21B, © Reinhard Dirscherl/Peter Arnold Inc.; 22T, © Brandon Cole Marine Photography/Alamy; 22B, © Charles Stirling/Alamy.

Publisher: Kenn Goin
Editorial Director: Adam Siegel
Creative Director: Spencer Brinker
Photo Researcher: James O'Connor
Design: Dawn Beard Creative

Library of Congress Cataloging-in-Publication Data

Lunis, Natalie.
  Portuguese man-of-war : floating misery / by Natalie Lunis.
    p. cm. — (Afraid of the water)
  Includes bibliographical references and index.
  ISBN-13: 978-1-59716-946-2 (library binding)
  ISBN-10: 1-59716-946-3 (library binding)
  1. Portuguese man-of-war—Juvenile literature. I. Title.

  QL377.H9L86 2010
  593.5'5—dc22
                              2009006406

For more information, write to Bearport Publishing Company, Inc., 101 Fifth Avenue, Suite 6R, New York, New York 10003. Printed in the United States of America.

10 9 8 7 6 5 4 3 2 1

Contents

A Bad Day at the Beach

Cameron Moeller was taking a swim off Clearwater Beach, Florida. As a lifeguard, he swam just about every day. A long workout in the water was part of his regular training.

Just as the six-foot-tall (1.8 m) lifeguard stretched out his arm to take another stroke, he touched something stringy. At first, it seemed like seaweed. Then Cameron felt the first sting—"like a hot knife going in," he later recalled. The dangling strings Cameron had touched weren't seaweed at all. They were part of something very different and very dangerous—a floating, stinging Portuguese man-of-war.

DANGER

The Portuguese man-of-war was named by sailors who had traveled the seas hundreds of years ago. Its shape reminded them of the sails on a warship that was built and used by the Portuguese navy.

A Portuguese man-of-war sailing ship

A Portuguese man-of-war
floating in the water

Tangled in Tentacles

Cameron had swum into a trap—a long, stringy mass of man-of-war **tentacles**. He swam toward **shore** to get away from the stinging strands. The more he moved, however, the more tangled he became. The tentacles were now wrapped around his arm, chest, and back.

Finally, Cameron ran onto the sand, still dragging the man-of-war with him. He pulled the tentacles off his skin, but he was feeling awful and having trouble breathing. Lifeguards helped Cameron get to a fire station for first aid. He was then sent to a hospital where he was given medicines to reduce the pain. Doctors told Cameron he was going to be fine, though he needed to take it easy for the next couple of days.

DANGER

After Cameron was stung, lifeguards at Clearwater Beach put up warning flags to keep people out of the water for the next few days.

Cameron Moeller, lifeguard at Clearwater Beach, Florida, showing scars that remained after being stung by a Portuguese man-of-war in May 2008

Not a Jellyfish

When Cameron first felt a hot burning pain in his hand, he thought he had been stung by a jellyfish. However, a Portuguese man-of-war is not a jellyfish—even though it looks like one.

A jellyfish is an animal that uses stinging tentacles to catch small sea animals for food. A Portuguese man-of-war also uses stinging tentacles to catch **prey**. However, it can't be called an animal—at least, not a single animal. Instead, a man-of-war is a **colony**, or group of animals that live together and depend on one another to survive.

Portuguese man-of-war

A man-of-war's long tentacles hang down into the water.

jellyfish

tentacles

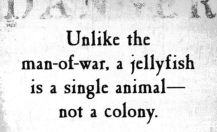

DANGER

Unlike the
man-of-war, a jellyfish
is a single animal—
not a colony.

Thousands of stingers on a
jellyfish's tentacles kill or stun
the fish that get caught in them.

Four Kinds in One

Four different kinds of **polyps** live in the colony that makes up a man-of-war. Each has a different job to do.

One kind of polyp acts as the **float**—the clear, balloon-like part of the man-of-war that keeps the entire colony from sinking. The other kinds of polyps hang down from the float. Some of these catch food. Others break the food down and pass it along to the rest of the colony. Still others are involved in **reproduction**. Their job is to make baby men-of-war.

float polyp

capturing, feeding, and reproductive polyps

DANGER

Altogether, there can be hundreds of polyps in a man-of-war colony. Only one polyp makes up the float. However, there are many of each of the other kinds.

10

A close-up view of the polyps that hang down from a man-of-war's float

11

Sailing Along

A Portuguese man-of war can't swim to get from one place to another. Instead, it **drifts** and bobs in the ocean where wind and water **currents** often move it over great distances.

The wind pushes the man-of-war along when it hits the sail-shaped ridge at the top of its float. When this "sail" catches the wind, a man-of-war can move at a speed of up to one mile per hour (1.6 kph). Currents in the water are even more powerful. They can carry a man-of-war at speeds of up to six miles per hour (9.7 kph).

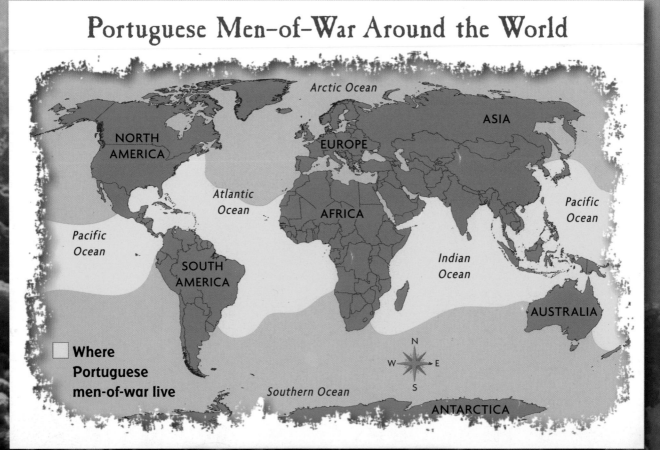

Portuguese Men-of-War Around the World

Arctic Ocean

ASIA

NORTH AMERICA

EUROPE

Atlantic Ocean

Pacific Ocean

AFRICA

Pacific Ocean

SOUTH AMERICA

Indian Ocean

AUSTRALIA

☐ **Where Portuguese men-of-war live**

Southern Ocean

ANTARCTICA

N
W E
S

This map shows the ocean waters where Portuguese men-of-war can be found.

A group of Portuguese men-of-war
floating in Australia

DANGER

Sometimes hundreds
of men-of-war come
together because they are
swept up by the same
current or winds.

These men-of war were
washed up on a beach.

13

Many Mouths to Feed

As a man-of-war drifts in the water, the long tentacles of its food-catching polyps hang down. Sometimes small fish, shrimp, and other sea creatures swim into them. That's when the man-of-war's tentacles release their **venom**.

Coiled up inside each tentacle are thousands of tiny stingers. They shoot the poison into a victim to **paralyze** it. Once the creature stops moving, the tentacles pull it up to the feeding polyps—each of which has a mouth that leads straight to a stomach. There, powerful juices break the food down into a form that the feeding polyps can pass on to the rest of the colony.

cobra

DANGER

A man-of-war's venom is nearly as powerful as that of a cobra—one of the deadliest snakes on Earth. However, since a man-of-war injects less venom than the bite of a cobra, its sting is less dangerous to a person.

A fish trapped in a Portuguese man-of-war's tentacles

Any Enemies?

The Portuguese man-of-war feeds on many kinds of creatures that live in the sea. Do any animals feed on the floating, stinging colony, though? Surprisingly, some do.

Several kinds of fish can take a bite out of a man-of-war. One of them, the 10-foot-long (3-m) ocean sunfish, can even swallow a man-of-war whole. Two large sea turtles—the loggerhead and the hawksbill—like to munch on men-of-war as well. Because of their hard shells and thick, leathery skin, the turtles are not hurt by the man-of-war's stings.

hawksbill turtle

ocean sunfish

violet sea snail

A violet sea snail attacking a Portuguese man-of-war

blue ocean slug

DANGER

Some small sea animals attack and eat men-of-war, too. They include the violet sea snail and the frilly-looking blue ocean slug.

Should You Be Afraid?

Portuguese men-of-war don't chase after people. They can go only where the wind and currents carry them. Usually, they drift around in the middle of the ocean, far from shore. Sometimes, however, they are carried closer to land. That's the time when people in the water need to be careful.

Swimmers, snorkelers, or surfers may not see a man-of-war's float nearby. Yet that doesn't mean they are safe. A man-of-war's tentacles are so long—up to 165 feet (50 m)—that a swimmer could brush against them and get stung without even seeing the float. Luckily, deaths from a man-of-war's stings are very, very rare.

Surfers sometimes get stung by a man-of-war as they head out toward the waves.

Although some men-of-war tentacles can be up to 165 feet (50 m) long, most are from 3 to 30 feet (1 to 9 m) long.

DANGER

Sometimes one or more of a man-of-war's tentacles break off from the rest of the colony. The broken-off tentacles are still able to sting as they drift around on their own.

19

Getting Help

Most people will never meet up with a man-of-war. Yet every year, some unlucky swimmers get stung. Fortunately, there are ways to ease the pain. Experts suggest these steps.

1. Remove any tentacles that are left on the skin. Wear gloves so you don't touch them with bare fingers.
2. Rinse the sting well with salt water.
3. Use ice to bring down any swelling.
4. If the victim has trouble breathing, feels dizzy, or has a fever, get medical help right away.

People can also take two important steps to stay away from the floating stingers in the first place. One is to swim only at beaches with lifeguards. Another is to obey safety signs that warn of men-of-war. After all, this is one form of sea life you don't want to tangle with!

DANGER

Sometimes the wind or waves wash Portuguese men-of-war onto beaches. People should never touch them, however. The tentacles can still sting after the float has dried out and died.

DANGER
MAN·O·WAR

This warning sign was posted on a beach in Hollywood, Florida.

21

Other Things That Sting

The Portuguese man-of-war is one ocean dweller that can deliver a dangerous sting. Other kinds of sea creatures also have powerful stings.

Southern Stingrays

- A southern stingray is a fish that has a large, flat, diamond-shaped body and a long, whip-like tail.
- There are one or more sharp stingers on its tail. The stingers release venom when the stingray swings its tail up to attack an enemy.
- Southern stingrays swim along the bottom of the ocean, hunting sea creatures such as clams, worms, small fish, shrimp, and crabs.
- People sometimes get stung when they step on a stingray. The pain from a sting can be very bad, and it can take a long time for the wound to heal.

Bristleworms

- A bristleworm is a kind of seaworm that lives in warm ocean waters. It is usually found under rocks and in coral reefs.
- The worms have venom in their hair-like bristles. If an enemy touches the worm, some of the bristles break off. They pierce the enemy's skin and release the venom.
- Snorkelers and swimmers are sometimes stung by the worms. The sting causes pain and burning but usually is not dangerous.

Glossary

colony (KOL-uh-nee) a group of animals that live together and depend on one another to survive

currents (KUR-uhnts) the movement of water in an ocean or river

drifts (DRIFTS) moves by being carried along by water or wind

float (FLOHT) the large balloon-like part of a Portuguese man-of-war that keeps it from sinking below the surface of the water

paralyze (PA-ruh-*lize*) to cause something to be unable to move

polyps (POL-ips) animals that live and work together to make up one Portuguese man-of-war

prey (PRAY) animals that are hunted by other animals for food

reproduction (*ree*-pruh-DUHK-shuhn) the act of producing babies

shore (SHOR) the land along the edge of a lake, river, or ocean

tentacles (TEN-tuh-kuhlz) parts that hang down from a Portuguese man-of-war and can sting other animals

venom (VEN-uhm) poison that some animals can send into the bodies of other animals through a bite or sting

Index

Bibliography

Coldrey, Jennifer, and David Shale. *The Man-of-War at Sea.* London: Methuen (1987).

Donila, Mike. "Man-of-War's Sting 'Like a Hot Knife,'" *St. Petersburg Times* (May 23, 2008).

Parker, Steve. *Sponges, Jellyfish, and Other Simple Animals.* Minneapolis, MN: Compass Point Books (2006).

Read More

Brennan, Joseph K. *Jellyfish and Other Stingers.* Chicago: World Book, Inc. (2003).

Earle, Sylvia A. *Sea Critters.* Washington, D.C.: National Geographic Society (2000).

McFee, Shane. *Jellyfish.* New York: Rosen (2008).

Learn More Online

To learn more about the Portuguese man-of-war, visit
www.bearportpublishing.com/AfraidoftheWater

About the Author

Natalie Lunis has written many science and nature books for children. She lives in the Hudson River Valley, just north of New York City.